CHRONICLES OF FAITH

JESUS

Dan Larsen

Illustrated by
Al Bohl

BARBOUR
PUBLISHING

Cover Illustration: Cory Godbey, Portland Studios, Inc.

Published by Barbour Publishing, Inc., P.O. Box 719, Uhrichsville, Ohio 44683, www.barbourbooks.com

Our mission is to publish and distribute inspirational products offering exceptional value and biblical encouragement to the masses.

Member of the
Evangelical Christian
Publishers Association

Printed in the United States of America.

JESUS

"Simon."

1

By the Lake

We had been fishing all morning, my brother Andrew and I, on Lake Galilee. Though our nets had been in the water for many hours, our catch was small. About midday we hauled in our nets and rowed to shore. There we sat in the boat, mending and washing our nets.

We had not been at this long when I heard someone call my name. "Simon." I looked up. On the shore stood a man I had never seen before. I started to ask how he knew me when he said,

"Follow me, Simon, and you, Andrew. From now on you will be fishers of men."

I never looked to Andrew. I did not know or care what he was thinking just then. I was looking at the man. He wore a robe that came to his ankles. By his powerful shoulders, I could see that he was a house builder. But his face! Such strength I have never seen in any man. Even more than this, there was such authority in his gaze and voice that as I looked at him, I could say nothing. His eyes shone like all the stars in the heavens and seemed to stare right through my eyes into the depths of my soul.

I will never forget what happened next. I stood in my boat with my net, the only things I had ever owned. Fishing was my only past and my only future. I had no desire to leave that life behind. But when the man on the shore said, "Follow me," I clambered out of my boat and splashed to shore. My heart was

"Follow me!"

pounding, my knees trembling. The man turned and walked down the shore. And I followed him like a child, not once looking back at my boat.

It was only then that I realized my brother Andrew was with me. He had felt the call—felt it deep in his heart—and he had obeyed, too.

The man walked along the shore—Andrew and I at his heels—until he came to two other brothers in their boat. "James and John," the man called, "come with me." At once, the men dropped their nets, climbed out of the boat, and came to us.

We followed this man throughout Galilee. Here and there, he called more men to him. Before long there were twelve of us. Over the next three years we would follow this man all over Judea. We would see and hear things such as we had never seen or heard before. We would see the sick made well, the lame walk, the deaf hear, the blind see, and the

"Come with me!"

dead raised to life. We would see the very kingdom of heaven come down to earth! The whole world—all that is in it and all that will ever be—would be changed forever by the life of this one man.

I saw and heard these things, I and the other eleven men with me those three years. Not only we twelve, but many, many people all through the land of Judea saw and heard. The stories that are told of this man are true. They are not tales of imagination. They are the accounts of those who were there, who saw, who heard, who knew. I was with him wherever he went for those three years. I came to understand who he was. I grew to love him with all my heart and soul and strength. And he gave me a new name. "You are Peter, the rock," he said. "And on this rock I will build my church."

He called us disciples. When he left us, he said, "Go into all the world and make everyone my disciples."

"You are Peter, the rock!"

I have not written of these things before. Now I write because I must tell this story—first what I heard from many people who knew him before I, then what I saw and heard for myself when I was with him. This is the story of Jesus Christ, the Son of God, the Savior of the world.

This is the story of Jesus Christ.

"My name is Gabriel."

2

ONE NIGHT IN BETHLEHEM

It began in the city of Nazareth when Herod was king of Judea. In Nazareth lived a young woman named Mary. She was not yet married but was engaged to a man named Joseph.

One night she was startled awake. There in her room stood an angel. "My name is Gabriel," he said. "Peace be with you. The Lord is with you and has richly blessed you." Mary was trembling.

"Do not fear," the angel said. "You will become pregnant and give birth to a son, and you will name him Jesus. He will be called the Son of God. And there will be no end to his kingdom."

"How can this be?" asked Mary. "I am not married. I am a virgin."

"God's power will come upon you," the angel said. "There is nothing that God cannot do."

"I am the Lord's servant," Mary said. "Let it be done to me as you have said."

It was many months before Joseph and Mary were to be married. Before that time, Joseph learned that Mary was pregnant. He decided to tell her privately that he would not marry her, since he did not wish her shame to be known to everyone.

But one night in a dream, an angel came to him and said, "Joseph, do not be afraid to take Mary as your wife. She has not shamed you. It is by the power of God that she is pregnant. She will have a son, whom you are to name Jesus, and he will save people

"Joseph, do not be afraid."

from their sins. This is the child spoken of by the prophet who said, 'Behold, the virgin shall bear a son, who will be called Immanuel, or God with us.'"

So Mary and Joseph were married. Soon after, Emperor Augustus of Rome ordered a census, a count of the people living in the huge Roman Empire. All the people had to return to the place of their birth to be registered for the census. Joseph and Mary had to go to the town of Bethlehem, where their families came from.

They came to Bethlehem late one night. The inns were all full. It was cold, and Mary was about to give birth. They found a small stable where some animals were kept, and there Mary gave birth to Jesus. She wrapped him in cloths and laid him in a manger.

In a pasture near Bethlehem, some shepherds were spending the night with their flocks. Just after

They came to Bethlehem late one night.

Jesus was born, an angel came to the shepherds and said, "I bring good news, which will bring great joy to all people. This very day in the city of David, your Savior was born, Christ the Lord. You will find a baby wrapped in cloths and lying in a manger."

And suddenly it became as bright as day. Great armies of angels joined the first angel. They all said, "Glory to God in the highest heaven, and peace on earth to those with whom he is pleased."

The shepherds hurried into Bethlehem, where they found the baby. They told Mary and Joseph what the angel said; then they returned to their flocks, singing and praising God.

After about two years, Mary and Joseph returned to Nazareth. There the child, Jesus, grew to manhood. He helped his father, who was a house builder. Jesus grew strong in body and in wisdom.

"Glory to God in the highest."

"Repent of your sins and be baptized!"

3

THE SON OF MAN

When Jesus was about thirty years old, a man named John came out of the wilderness near Jerusalem. "Repent of your sins and be baptized!" he cried to the people. He went to the Jordan River, south of Lake Galilee, where he baptized people in the water. Many people came to him. "He is the Lord's holy prophet!" they said.

We fishermen of Lake Galilee began hearing of John—John the Baptist, as he was called. "Could he be the Messiah?" people asked. When John heard this, he answered, "I am not the one you are looking for. I baptize you in the water for repentance. But there is one coming after me who is so much mightier that I am not worthy to tie his sandals. He will baptize you in the Holy Spirit and in fire. I am only the one the prophet Isaiah spoke of when he said, 'Someone is shouting in the desert. Prepare a road for the Lord! Make a straight path for him to travel!' The one coming after me will gather his wheat into his barn, but he will burn the chaff in a fire that never goes out."

Then Jesus came to the Jordan. When John saw him, he said, "I should be baptized by you. Yet you have come to me!"

"Let it be so," said Jesus. "We must do all that God requires."

So John baptized him. Just as Jesus came out of the water, he saw heaven open, and God's Spirit

"You are my own dear Son, in whom I have delighted!"

came down to him in the form of a dove that rested on him. Then a voice said, "You are my own dear Son, in whom I have delighted."

Now the Spirit of God led Jesus into the desert. There he stayed, praying day and night. He ate no food all this time. After forty days, Satan came to him and said, "If you are the Son of God, command these stones to turn into bread."

Jesus said, "It is written, 'Man cannot live on bread alone but needs every word that God speaks.'"

Then Satan took Jesus to the top of a tall mountain. There he said, "Do you see all those kingdoms below? I will give you all those if you kneel down and worship me."

Jesus said, "Get away from me, Satan! It is written: 'Worship the Lord your God and serve only him.'"

"If you are the Son of God, jump off from here!"

Then Satan said, "Come with me." He led Jesus to Jerusalem, where he climbed to the top of the temple. Then Satan said, "If you are the Son of God, jump off from here! For it is written, 'God will command his angels to guard you. They will hold you up so that not even your feet will be hurt on the stones.'"

Jesus replied, "It is also written, 'Do not put the Lord your God to the test.'"

Hearing this, Satan fled over the desert. Jesus was very weak from having gone so long without food, but angels came to him and helped him down the mountain.

He went to live in a city called Capernaum, near Lake Galilee. Now filled with the Spirit and power of God, he began to preach to the people in the synagogues. "Turn away from your sins," he said. "The kingdom of heaven is near."

"Turn away from your sins."

"They have no wine."

4

His Authority

It was then that he came to us on Lake Galilee. We followed him into the synagogues, where he spoke of a coming kingdom. We did not understand everything, but we were drawn to him. There was power in every word he spoke. People listened to him in amazement. "He speaks with such authority!" we heard people say. "We have never heard anything like this!"

Three days after Jesus had come to us at Lake Galilee, we went to the city of Cana, where we had been invited to a wedding. The house was full of people, and Jesus' mother was there. Before long, she came to Jesus. "They have no more wine," she said.

"Why have you told me this?" he asked quietly. "My time has not yet come."

Andrew and I looked at each other. What did this mean?

Then Jesus' mother turned away and said to the servants of the house, "Do whatever he tells you." The servants came to Jesus, waiting for him to speak.

Finally he pointed to six stone water jars, each holding about thirty gallons. "Fill those with water," he said. "Then draw some out and take it to the man in charge of the feast."

We watched as a servant dipped some water out and went to the man. The servant said something

His eyes went wide.

to the man, then handed the dipper to him. As the man took a sip, his eyes went wide. He stared at the servant, then at the dipper, then at the stone jars. He beamed and clapped the servant on the back. Now the man walked over to the bridegroom, who was standing near us. "Sire," the man said, "everyone else serves the best wine first, and the cheapest after everyone has drunk freely. But you have saved the best wine until now!"

No one except the servants and we disciples knew where this wine had come from. We were so astounded we could hardly speak. "Who is this man?" we said to one another. "He must be sent from God! No man could have this power, if it were not given him by God himself."

After this wedding, we went with Jesus and his mother and brothers to Capernaum and stayed there for a few days. The days of the Passover

"Who is this man?"

festival were drawing near, and we were going to travel to Jerusalem to celebrate this festival.

In Jerusalem the first thing Jesus did was go to the temple, the holy place of Jerusalem, the place of worship. But we were not prepared for what we saw inside!

There were cattle and sheep and cages filled with pigeons and tables filled with coins throughout the temple. People were everywhere. Men were crying out, "Buy here! Buy here!" The din of bickering and squabbling echoed off the tall stone pillars and walls, as in a hollow cavern.

Jesus stopped short on seeing this. His eyes glinted like steel as he looked around, his fists clenched. Then he moved. He wrenched a cord of rope from a heavy curtain. Using this as a whip, he drove the cattle and sheep across the floor and out of the temple. Bawling and bleating, the animals

Cleansing the temple

stampeded toward the doors. Men screamed and ran for safety.

Then Jesus grabbed the massive wooden tables and flung them to the floor with a fury that seemed to crack the very stone under his feet. Silver and gold coins rang across the floor.

No one tried to stop him. All stood wide-eyed and openmouthed as this powerful figure cleared the temple. Soon it was still.

Jesus pointed at the sellers. His voice boomed in the now silent temple. "This is my Father's house," he said, "but you have made it a hideout for thieves!"

The priest and the teachers of the Law were in the temple. They were furious with Jesus, but now a crowd was gathering. People poured in through the doors. They had seen the stampeding animals and were curious. A murmur rose up among the

"This is my Father's house!"

people, then grew to a roar. "Praise the God of the heavens!" they shouted. "This man comes in the name of God!"

The priests stayed in the shadows of the temple, afraid of Jesus and the excitement he stirred up among the people. They did not dare say a word.

During the days of the Passover festival, Jesus taught in the temple, and many came to him to be healed. With just a word he healed all their diseases. More and more people came into the temple, many of them saying that Jesus was the Messiah, the Promised One. But fear and hatred grew in the priests and the teachers.

One teacher, though, must have heard something in the words of Jesus that made him hunger to know more. He came to the house where we stayed one night. "I am Nicodemus," he said to Jesus. "I am a leader of the Pharisees. We know that

"I am Nicodemus."

you are a teacher who has come from God, for no one could do the miracles you have done unless he had the power of God."

"I tell you the truth," Jesus said, "unless a man be born again, he cannot see the kingdom of God."

Nicodemus frowned. "How can a man be born again?" he asked.

"You must be born of water and the Spirit," Jesus said. "You are born physically from human parents, but you must be born spiritually by the Spirit. The wind blows wherever it wishes, and you listen to its sound, but you know not where it comes from or where it is going. It is like that with everyone who is born of the Spirit."

"How can this be?" asked Nicodemus.

"You are a teacher of Israel," Jesus said, "and you do not know this? You teachers do not believe me when I tell you about the things of this world. How

will you ever believe me when I tell you about the things of heaven?

"As Moses lifted up the bronze snake in the desert, so must the Son of Man be lifted up, so that everyone who believes in him may have life eternal. For God loved the world so much that he gave his only Son, so that whoever believes in him should not die but have eternal life."

Nicodemus went away into the night, puzzled over what Jesus had said.

When the Passover festival was over, we left Jerusalem and went into the countryside, where Jesus baptized many people in the Jordan. After two days we went to Cana in Galilee, where Jesus had turned the water into wine. Here the people recognized Jesus, for many of them had been to the festival in Jerusalem. Word of Jesus' teaching and

"Sir, my son is dying."

around us as we walked through the dusty streets.

We had been there a few days when a court officer from Capernaum came to see Jesus one evening. This man was wringing his hands. "Sir," he said, "my son is dying. Please come with me before it is too late."

"Go," Jesus said. "Your son lives!"

A look of wonder came over the man's face. He straightened his shoulders. "I believe!" he said. "I will go, as you say."

We later learned that the boy became well at that very hour. The man and all his family believed in Jesus.

5

HIS WISDOM

We traveled to Capernaum, where Jesus went into the synagogue on the Sabbath to teach. One of those days as Jesus was teaching the crowd, a man came forward. We all drew back in terror at the sight of him. His eyes were blazing with a strange fire. His lips were twisted in a bestial grin. Suddenly he screamed, "What do you want with us, Jesus of Nazareth? Have you come to destroy us? I know who you are. You are the Holy One of God!"

The crowd was hushed. Everyone stared in horror at this raging man. Jesus stood in front of him. The man was shaking and foaming at the mouth. His hands clutched like talons at the empty air. He seemed ready to erupt, like a volcano. We gasped. What would he do? Attack Jesus?

But Jesus pointed straight at the man. The man threw his head back as if to let out another shriek. "Be still!" came Jesus' voice. There was danger in those words, as sharp as a sword. The man suddenly stood as if he were locked in a vise. Then Jesus said, "Come out of him!"

Suddenly the man fell to the floor, as if thrown by invisible hands. Jesus helped him up. Now the man sobbed and praised God. The evil look in his eyes was gone.

Shouts of praise went up from the crowd, and many people stared in wonder at Jesus. "What

The man sobbed and praised God.

authority and power are in his words!" we heard some say. "He commands, and even evil spirits tremble before him and obey! Praise the name of God!"

People went everywhere and told of Jesus. His fame spread like fire through the whole region. We went all through Galilee, where Jesus taught in the synagogues. Many people came to believe in him. He healed the sick, made the blind see and the lame walk, and cast out evil spirits. In every city we entered, the people thronged around us to see Jesus and hear him speak.

We began to stay out in the wilderness so we could have some peace from the crowds. But even in the wilderness, the people found and followed us. They came from Galilee and the Decapolis, and from Jerusalem and all of Judea, even from Syria.

Jesus prayed all night.

One day Jesus went up a mountain alone. He stayed there all night praying. Very early the next morning, he woke us. Of the men following him, he appointed twelve to be his apostles, or disciples. He appointed me—Simon—my brother Andrew, the brothers James and John—who were the sons of Zebedee—Philip, Bartholomew, Thomas, Matthew, James the son of Alphaeus, Judas Thaddaeus, Simon of Cana, and Judas Iscariot.

Then he took the twelve of us to the top of the mountain, told us to sit down, and began to teach us.

"Happy are you who mourn, for God will comfort you.

"Happy are you who are humble, for you will receive what God has promised.

"Happy are you who show mercy, for God will show mercy to you.

The Beatitudes

"Happy are you who are pure in heart, for you will see God.

"Happy are you who work for peace, for God will call you his children.

"Happy are you who are persecuted for doing what God requires, for the kingdom of heaven belongs to you.

"Happy are you when people insult you and tell lies about you because you are my followers. Be happy and glad, for a great reward is kept for you in heaven. This is how the prophets who lived before you were persecuted."

The morning passed, the afternoon came, and still we sat with Jesus. His face shone as he spoke to us.

"You are like light for the world," he said. "And no one lights a lamp and puts it under a bowl. Instead, he puts it on a lampstand, where it gives

"You are like light for the world."

light for everyone in the house. In the same way, your light must shine before people, so they will see the good things you do and praise your Father in heaven.

"Do not think I have come to do away with the Law of Moses and the teachings of the prophets. I have arrived to make their teachings come true. Remember that as long as heaven and earth last, not the smallest detail of the Law will be done away with—not until the end of all things. You will be able to enter the kingdom of heaven only if you are more faithful than the teachers of the Law and the Pharisees in doing what God requires.

"You have been told that anyone who commits murder will be brought to trial. But now I tell you that whoever is angry with his brother will be brought to trial; whoever says to his brother, 'You good-for-nothing!' will be brought before the Council; and

Jesus teaching

whoever says to his brother, 'You worthless fool!' will be in danger of going to hell. So if you are about to offer a gift to God at the altar and you remember that your brother has something against you, go at once and make peace with your brother, and then come back and offer your gift to God.

"You have been told to not commit adultery. But now I tell you that anyone who lusts for a woman is guilty of committing adultery with her in his heart.

"You have heard it said, 'An eye for an eye, and a tooth for a tooth.' But now I tell you, do not take revenge on someone who wrongs you. If someone slaps you on the right cheek, let him slap you on the left cheek also. And if someone sues you for your shirt, let him have your coat as well.

"When you give something to a needy person, do not make a show of it. Do it privately so that

"Anyone who lusts for a woman is guilty."

even your closest friend will not know. And your Father, who sees what you do in private, will reward you. And when you pray, do not stand in the streets. Go to your room, close the door, and pray to your Father, who is unseen. And do not use a lot of meaningless words. Your Father already knows what you need. This, then, is how you should pray: 'Our Father in heaven, may your holy name be honored. May your kingdom come. May your will be done on earth as it is in heaven. Give us today the food we need. Forgive us the wrongs we have done, and we forgive the wrongs that others do to us. Keep us from temptation, and keep us safe from the Evil One.'"

Every word Jesus spoke became etched in my heart forever.

"His words became etched in my heart."

The widow's only child was dead.

6

His Power

When we came down from the mountain, we were met by great crowds of people who followed us into Capernaum, where we stayed that night. The next morning we set out for the city of Nain. We left Capernaum very early and walked all day. Toward evening we came to the city gates of Nain.

As we were about to enter, a large crowd of people came out from the city. Many of them wept. On the men's shoulders was a young boy stretched out on a bier, his face as pale as death. A woman walked beside the bier, wailing aloud.

We asked one of the men what had happened. "This woman's only child has died," he said sadly. "She is a widow and has no one left."

When Jesus heard this, a tender look came over his face. He looked at the woman as if he would weep, too. He walked toward the bier. "Do not weep," he said. Everyone stopped. They stared at Jesus as he came up to the dead boy. "Young man," Jesus said, "I tell you, get up!"

A gasp went up from the crowd. The boy was sitting up! "A great prophet has appeared!" came a shout. "God has come to save his people!" The woman held her son tightly as great sobs of joy shook her.

This story spread quickly throughout that region. We went with Jesus to city after city. We were followed everywhere. In the cities we were

Great sobs of joy shook her.

so pressed by crowds that sometimes we could not even sit down to eat. More and more, Jesus would go to Lake Galilee and sit in a boat just offshore to speak to the crowds. He would speak in parables. Many people would only wonder what he meant, but others understood.

"Once there was a man who went out to sow grain," Jesus said. "As he scattered the seed, some of it fell along the path, where the birds ate it. Some fell on rocky ground. The seed soon sprouted, but because the soil was shallow, the plants did not grow deep roots and were burned by the sun. Some seed fell among thornbushes, which grew up and choked the plants. But some seed fell in good soil and bore grain. Some had a hundred grains, others sixty, and others thirty. Listen, then, if you have ears."

When the crowds had left, we disciples asked

"A man went out to sow grain."

Jesus why he spoke to the people only in parables. He answered, "Because these people look, but do not see, and listen, but do not hear or understand. The prophet Isaiah spoke of these people when he said, 'They will listen, but not understand. They will look but not see because their minds are dull, and they have stopped up their ears and have closed their eyes. Otherwise their eyes would see, their ears would hear, their minds would understand, and they would turn to me, says God, and I would heal them.'

"As for you," Jesus said, "your eyes see and your ears hear. This is what the parable of the sower means. Those who hear my message but do not understand are like the seeds that fell on the path. The Evil One comes and snatches away what was sown there. The seeds that fell on the rocky ground are those who receive the message gladly as soon

"Some people close their eyes and ears
to the truth."

as they hear it. But it does not last long. When trouble comes, they give up at once. The seeds that fell among the thornbushes are those who hear the message but allow the worries of life and the love of riches to choke the message. And the seeds sown in good soil are those who hear and understand. They are the ones who bear fruit."

Jesus told many other parables. "The kingdom of heaven is like a mustard seed," he said. "It is the smallest of seeds, but it grows into the biggest of plants. It becomes a tree, so that birds make their nests in its branches.

"The kingdom of heaven is like this: A woman takes some yeast and mixes it with a bushel of flour until the whole batch of dough rises.

"The kingdom of heaven is like this: A man is looking for fine pearls. When he finds one that is unusually fine, he goes and sells everything he

The pearl of great price

has and buys that pearl.

"The kingdom of heaven is like this: Fishermen throw their net out and catch all kinds of fish. When the net is full, they pull it to shore and sit down to divide the fish. The good ones go into buckets, and the worthless ones are thrown away. It will be like this at the end of the age. The angels will go out and gather up the evil people from among the good and will throw them into the fire."

When it began to grow dark, we disciples sent the crowds home. Then we were alone with Jesus. We all got into the boat with him to go to the other side of the lake. Jesus quickly fell asleep in the boat. About halfway across, the wind picked up and the waves rose. Soon we were in a violent windstorm. The waves began washing over the sides of the boat. We worked frantically to keep the boat afloat, bailing out water and bracing ourselves against the

A violent windstorm arose!

smashing waves. All through this, Jesus slept.

Now we were sure we would be drowned. I shook Jesus. "Master!" I cried. "Do you not care that we are about to drown?"

Jesus awoke and frowned at me. "Why are you afraid?" he asked. "Where is your faith?" Then he stood up in the pitching boat. We all stared at him in wonder. His voice came like thunder. "Be still!"

Immediately the wind stopped. A great calm settled over the water. Jesus easily went back to sleep again.

"Who is this man?" we said. "Even the winds and waves obey his commands!" And I wondered if there was anything he couldn't do.

"Be still!"

"I have been sick for many years."

7

The Son of God

Soon we went to Jerusalem to celebrate a feast of the Jews. In Jerusalem we came upon a man lying on a mat by the street. He seemed very ill. Jesus said, "You have been here long."

The man stared up at Jesus. "How did you know that?" he asked. "I have been sick for many years. I cannot walk very far. I am too weak."

Jesus' face shone with a soft light. "Get up!" he said to the man. "Pick up your mat and walk."

The man's eyes opened wide, but he took a

deep breath and stood up. He stared at Jesus open-mouthed, and tears came to his eyes. Slowly he picked up his mat and walked away, speechless.

People were staring. "Quickly," Jesus said. We got away before a crowd could gather.

About two days later the priests from the temple came to us. Their faces were grave as they spoke to Jesus. "On the past Sabbath we saw a man carrying his sleeping mat," they said. "When we told him it is against the Law to carry his mat on a Sabbath, he said that a certain man told him to carry it."

One of the priests pointed at Jesus. The priest was bristling. "That man was you!" he said. "You are a Jew. Have you no regard for our Law?"

Jesus said, "My Father is always working, and I, too, must work."

"Your father!" said a priest through clenched

"That man was you!"

teeth. "You are saying God is your father. For this you deserve death!"

The priests gathered in front of Jesus, their fists clenched, their faces flushed. But they cowered together in a knot, as a pack of hounds before a lion.

Though Jesus spoke calmly, his words seemed to fly through the air like arrows toward the group of priests. "I tell you the truth," Jesus said. "The Son does only what he sees his Father doing. For the Father loves the Son and shows him even greater things to do than this. You will be amazed. Just as the Father raises the dead and gives them life, in the same way the Son gives life to those he wants to. Nor does the Father himself judge anyone." Here Jesus looked sharply at the priests. "He has given his Son the full right to judge. And whoever does not honor the Son does not honor the Father who sent him. I am telling you the truth. Whoever hears my words and believes

"You deserve death!"

in him who sent me has eternal life. He will not be judged, but has already passed from death to life. The Father himself testifies on my behalf. You have never heard his voice or seen his face, and you do not keep his message in your hearts, for you do not believe in the one he sent. You study the scriptures, because you think that in them you will find eternal life. And these very scriptures speak about me! Yet you are not willing to come to me in order to have life."

This made the priests all the more furious, but they said nothing.

Soon we left Jerusalem and went north to Nazareth. From there we went north again and sailed across Lake Galilee to a wilderness region outside the city of Bethsaida. Here Jesus hoped to rest for a little while.

But somehow people knew we had come. Even

"The scriptures speak about me!"

in the wilderness, they flocked to Jesus like lost sheep. They brought their sick and lame and blind. Jesus healed many, many people that day. Then he spoke to them about the kingdom of heaven.

The day passed, and night came. Jesus drew us disciples aside. "Where can we get food for these people?" he asked. As I looked at him, I wondered if he already knew the answer.

Philip said, "Master, there must be five thousand men here, not counting the women and children. All we have are two small fish and five loaves of bread!"

"It is already late," Jesus said. "These people have not had food all day. We cannot send them away. No, you give them food yourselves. Bring the fish and bread to me. Then have the people sit down in groups of about fifty."

We did as he said. He took the fish and bread,

"All we have are two small fish
and five loaves of bread!"

gave thanks for them, and broke the loaves, putting the pieces in baskets. We went among the groups, passing out the baskets, and we could not believe our eyes! Everyone took as much food as they wanted from the baskets, and there seemed no end to the supply! When everyone had eaten, Jesus told us to gather up what was left, so that nothing would be wasted. When we did, we found that we had twelve baskets full of pieces!

Then Jesus sent us ahead of him in the boat to the other side of the lake, saying he would join us there later.

We set out, rowing toward Capernaum. Soon it grew dark and a storm rose. The wind blew against us. We strained at the oars, fighting the wind. Our boat foundered in the waves. How could Jesus follow us now? One man in a boat would be helpless in this wind.

Jesus fed over 5,000 people.

We had been at this for hours when suddenly someone pointed out across the stormy water. "A ghost!" he screamed. We looked, and our hearts froze!

There, off in the blackness of the night, we saw a figure in white coming toward us. It looked like a man. But there was no boat! We just stared, too terrified to move or speak. The figure came on. Now we could see that, yes, it was a man. He was walking as if along a street, right over the thrashing waves. He drew nearer and nearer. Suddenly someone shouted, "It is the Lord!"

"Courage!" came a familiar voice. "It is I." Now he was quite close. It did indeed look like Jesus. But was it really a ghost?

"Lord," I said, my voice shaking, "if it is really you, tell me to come to you."

"Come then, Simon," he said.

"A ghost!"

My heart pounding, I stepped onto the water. And stood! Then I began walking toward Jesus. Suddenly I realized what I was doing. I stopped. The wind howled around me. I looked down. Below me were the inky depths of the lake, the waves rolling under my feet. Terror seized me as I saw the water rising up over my feet, up my legs, past my waist. "Lord, save me!" I gasped, reaching out.

I felt his strong hand on my arm, pulling me up as if I were a doll. He led me to the boat. "Why did you doubt?" he asked.

Now we all bowed to Jesus. "Truly you are the Son of God!" we said.

"Lord, save me!"

Large crowds followed Jesus.

8

REJECTION AND DESERTION

The crowds followed us even across the lake. That day many people from Bethsaida came in boats and found us in Capernaum.

Jesus said, "You seek me not because you saw miracles, but because you ate the fish and bread I gave you. Do not work for food that spoils, but for the food that lasts for eternal life. This is the food the Son of Man will give you."

"What is the work that God requires of us?" they asked.

"That you believe in the one he sent," said Jesus.

"What sign, what miracle, can you give us so we can believe in you?" they asked. "Moses gave our ancestors manna—bread from heaven—to eat in the desert. What will you do?"

"Moses did not give you the bread from heaven," Jesus said. "My Father gives you the real bread from heaven. This bread gives life."

"Give us this bread!" they said.

"I am the bread of life," Jesus said. "He who comes to me will never be hungry. If anyone eats this bread, he will live forever. The bread that I will give him is my flesh, which I give so that the world may live."

At this the people started arguing. "How can this man give us his flesh to eat?" some said.

"I am the bread of life."

Jesus said, "The words that I speak to you are spirit and life. Yet some of you do not believe. This is the reason I have said that no one can come to me unless my Father makes it possible."

On hearing this, many of Jesus' followers turned back. Jesus turned to us twelve. "What about you?" he asked. "Do you wish to leave, too?"

"Lord," I said, "where would we go? You have the words of eternal life. And now we believe and know that you are the Holy One who has come from God."

After this we traveled only in the region of Galilee for a while. We stayed out of Judea because the Jews there wanted to kill Jesus. In Galilee many people came to Jesus in the wilderness areas. He healed the sick and cast out many demons.

Now the Jewish Feast of the Tabernacles drew

"Lord, you have the words of eternal life."

near. We went to Jerusalem for this feast, traveling mostly at night, so we could go about unseen. Jesus did not wish to be recognized until the day of the feast.

On the first day of the feast, Jesus entered the temple and began teaching. Immediately the people recognized him. The priests did not dare to arrest Jesus, because they were afraid of the people.

But even the people seemed divided over Jesus. "Is he not the one the rulers are trying to kill?" someone asked. "Look. Here he is, speaking openly, and they say nothing of him! Have the rulers also come to believe that he is the Messiah?"

"How can he be the Messiah?" others said. "We know that when the Messiah comes, no one will know where he is from. Yet we know where this man is from."

The people were divided over Jesus.

Jesus said to them, "Do you know me, and where I am from? You do not know the one who sent me, but I know him, because I came from him, and he sent me."

Some in the crowd now shouted, "Seize him! This is blasphemy!" But others said, "When the Messiah comes, will he do more than this man has done?" Still others said, "He is the holy prophet!" and "He is the Messiah!" And the argument went on like this all day.

We left the temple, and Jesus went to the Mount of Olives, where he spent the night. Early the next morning he went back to the temple. People gathered to hear him teach.

"I am the light of the world," Jesus said. "Whoever follows me will have the light of life and will never walk in darkness."

"Seize him!"

Some Pharisees now came up to him. "You are testifying on your own behalf," they said. "So your testimony means nothing."

Jesus asked, "It is not written in your Law that when two witnesses agree, what they say is true? I testify on my own behalf, and my Father testifies on my behalf."

"Where is your father?" they asked.

"If you knew me, you would know my Father also," Jesus said.

"Our father is Abraham!" the Pharisees said.

"If Abraham really were your father, you would do the same things he did," said Jesus. "All I have ever done is tell you the truth, and for this you want to kill me. Abraham did nothing like this! You are doing what your real father does."

"Our father is God himself," they said.

"I tell the truth, and you want to kill me!"

"If God were your father, you would love me," Jesus said, "because I came from God. Why do you not understand what I say? It is because you cannot bear to listen to my message. You are the children of your father, the Devil, and you want to follow your father's desires.

"From the very beginning he was a murderer and a liar. When he lies, it is from his own nature that he speaks, for he is the father of all lies. Yet because I tell you the truth, you do not believe me. Anyone who is truly a child of God would believe my words. And my words are that whoever believes in me will never die."

"You have a demon!" the Pharisees said. "Abraham himself died. Do you claim to be greater than he?"

"I make no claim to honor myself," Jesus said. "It

"You have a demon!"

is my Father who seeks to honor me. But I tell you the truth, Abraham rejoiced that he was to see the time of my coming."

"You are not yet fifty years old!" they said. "And Abraham has seen you?"

"Before Abraham was born, I am," Jesus said.

At this the Pharisees tried to grab him, but Jesus simply got up and walked out of the temple.

The Pharisees tried to grab him.

"You are the Messiah."

9

THE MESSIAH

After we left Jerusalem, we went far north, to the city of Caesarea Philippi. Our journey took many days. One morning on this journey, Jesus went off alone to pray. He often did this, many times staying away all night, but this day he soon returned. "Tell ___ "who do men say that I am?"

___ say John the Baptist; oth-
___miah or some other

The words came out of my mouth before I really thought about them. "You are the Messiah," I said, "the Son of the living God."

Jesus said, "Blessed are you, Simon, son of Jonah! For this truth did not come to you from any human being, but from my Father in heaven. So I tell you that you are Peter, the rock, just as I am the Rock, the solid foundation on which everything of God was made. And on this rock I will build my church. And against this church the gates of hell will not prevail! I will give you, Peter, the keys of the kingdom of heaven, and everything you bind or loose on earth will be bound or loosed in heaven."

As we walked, Jesus spoke plain⌁ what would happen to him. "⌁ suffer greatly," he said ⌁

"You are Peter, the rock."

This thought shook me. How could it be? I learned only after Jesus' death what he had meant that day. But now I stopped him in the road. "Lord!" I said. "This must never happen to you!"

Jesus looked straight into my eyes. He seemed to be staring past me, though, to something beyond me. "Get away from me, Satan!" he said. "This is not God's thought, but man's. You are an obstacle in the path that my Father has chosen for me!"

Then Jesus said, "If someone wants to come after me, he must forget himself, carry his cross daily, and follow me. Whoever seeks to save his own life will lose it, but whoever loses his life for my sake will find it. For what will a person gain who wins the whole world but loses his life?"

It was six days after this that I saw Jesus' glory revealed. I will never forget the sight! One morning he woke me and asked me to go with him up a tall

"Jesus looked straight into my eyes."

mountain nearby. He also called the brothers James and John. We climbed to the top in the growing daylight.

At the top we all knelt down and prayed. Or at least Jesus prayed. I did not really know how to pray yet. Soon Jesus went off by himself. As we watched him kneeling, suddenly he seemed to burst into flames. His face and clothes were whiter than anything I had ever seen. And now as we stared, two other men suddenly appeared. They too were clothed in brightness. Jesus talked with these two.

Somehow I knew who these men were, even though no one told me. I was so shaken that I did not know what to do or say. "Lord," I stammered, "it is good that we disciples are here. We will make three shelters, one for you, one for Moses, and one for Elijah."

But just as I said this, a great light appeared

Two other men suddenly appeared.

overhead. We looked up and saw a cloud as white as Jesus and the two men. And a voice came from the cloud, saying, "This is my own dear Son, with whom I am pleased. Listen to him!"

James, John, and I fell to our faces on the ground, trembling. "Get up," came Jesus' voice. "Do not be afraid." We looked up. Jesus was alone. The other men and the cloud were gone. "Do not tell anyone what you have seen here," Jesus said, "until the Son of Man has been raised from death."

The crowds still came to us and followed Jesus, but there were fewer people now, and many of them began asking Jesus to prove himself. "Show us a sign," they would say.

This grieved Jesus. "The only sign you will be given is the sign of Jonah," he said. "Just as Jonah spent three days in the belly of a fish, so shall the Son of Man spend three days in the depths of the

"Show us a sign."

earth, to be raised to life on the third day."

Jesus began spending more time alone with us disciples. He taught us about the kingdom of God, explaining things to us in plain words.

One day as we walked in the streets of Capernaum, we disciples were arguing about who among us was the greatest. Jesus came up to us. "Sit down, all of you," he said. We sat by the side of the street, and Jesus sat with us. "Why were you arguing about who is the greatest?" he asked. We were too ashamed to answer.

"If anyone wishes to be the first, he must be last of all," Jesus said. Then he called a little girl who was walking by. She came to him shyly. Tenderly he took her in his arms. I had never seen my Lord's face so full of love. His eyes shone.

"Whoever humbles himself as this little child here will be great in heaven," he said. "I tell you,

His eyes shone.

unless you become like little children, you will never enter the kingdom of heaven. And whoever receives a child like this in my name also receives not only me but my Father.

"What do you think a man does who has a hundred sheep and loses one?" Jesus continued. "He will leave the others and look for the lost sheep. When he finds it, he is far happier with it than with the ninety-nine that were not lost. In the same way, your Father in heaven does not want any of these little ones to be lost."

Soon after this, in the city of Bethany, we were invited to the home of two sisters, Martha and Mary. All day Mary sat with Jesus, asking him questions and listening to his words.

Toward evening, Martha came to Jesus. She was angry. "Lord, do you not care that my sister has left me to do all the preparation?" she asked. "Tell her

Martha was angry.

to come and help me!"

Jesus took Martha by the hand. "Martha, Martha," he said. "You are troubled about many things. But only one thing is needed, and Mary has chosen the best thing. This cannot be taken away from her."

During these days, many Pharisees came in groups to see Jesus. They tried to trap him with questions, hoping he would say something against their Law. They wished for nothing more than to have him arrested and killed. Many, many people saw the truth about how the Pharisees lied and cheated for their own gain, how they used religion simply to satisfy their selfish desires. And Jesus had hard words for the Pharisees.

"You Pharisees clean the outside of your cup," he said, "but inside you are full of violence and evil. Fools! Did not God, who made the outside, also make the inside?

"You Pharisees only clean the outside of the cup."

"How terrible for you Pharisees! You give God a tenth of your seasonings and herbs, but you neglect justice and love for God.

"How terrible for you Pharisees! You love the best seats in the synagogues and to be greeted with respect in the marketplaces. You are like white-washed tombs. Outside you look clean, but inside you are full of bones and filth.

"How terrible for you teachers! You put heavy loads on the backs of the people to whom you teach the Law. But you yourselves will not even lift a finger to help these people carry those loads. You teachers have kept the key that opens the door to knowledge. But you yourselves will not enter, and you stop those who are trying to enter."

Jesus was criticized bitterly for saying these things, but the Pharisees and teachers never trapped

"You put heavy loads on people's backs."

him with their questions. Eventually no one dared ask him any more questions. In his answers, he spoke only the truth, and his accusers could not hear the truth.

They never trapped Jesus with questions.

"I will be tortured and killed."

10

THE LAST JOURNEY

We began to make our way slowly toward Jerusalem, going through all the cities and villages along the way. It would be the last time he would ever entered Jerusalem, Jesus told us. He told us again how the Son of Man would be handed over to the rulers and would be tortured and killed.

In the cities and villages, Jesus continued to heal all who came to him and to teach the crowds who gathered. He did not go into the synagogues now, though. All the leaders of the Jewish religion were against him. So people came to him in the streets, in the village squares, on the roads between cities, and even in the wilderness.

One day we sat outside a village among a group of people. A man asked Jesus, "Lord, will only a few be saved?"

Jesus said, "Try to enter the narrow door, because many will try but will not be able. The master of the house will shut the door, and you will knock outside saying, 'Lord, Lord, open the door for us.' He will answer, 'I do not know you.' And you will say, 'We ate bread with you. You taught in the streets of our city.' But he will answer, 'I do not know where you come from. Get away from me, you wicked people!' People will come from the east and west, from the north and south, and sit down at the feast in the kingdom of God. Then those who are now last will be first, and those who are now first will be last."

"People came from everywhere to feast."

One evening I went with Jesus to a Pharisee's home. We had been invited there to dinner. As we ate, Jesus spoke to the other dinner guests. "When you give a banquet, do not invite your friends or relatives," he said. "Invite the poor, the lame, and the blind, because they cannot pay you back. You will be paid for the good things you do on the day of resurrection."

One of the guests then said, "How happy are those who will sit down at the feast in the kingdom of God!"

Jesus said, "There was once a man who was giving a great feast to which he had invited many people. When it was time for the feast, he sent his servants to bring his guests, but his guests began making excuses for not coming. One by one they refused the invitation. The servants went back and told their master that no one would come. The

They refused the invitation.

master said to the servants, 'Hurry into the streets and bring back the poor, the crippled, the blind. And go to the country roads and invite everyone in, so my house will be full. But I tell you that none of those who were first invited will taste my dinner!' "

Soon after this, we were walking on a road in Samaria when we were met by ten men with leprosy, a terrible skin disease. They recognized Jesus. "Jesus, master, have mercy on us!" they cried.

Jesus said, "Go to the priest and have him examine you, according to the Law."

They quickly went down the road. Shortly after, one of them came running up to us again. He knelt in the road at Jesus' feet and thanked him. Then he stood up. His skin had been blotchy and discolored, but now it was clear and healthy.

"There were ten of you," Jesus said. "And yet

"Jesus, have mercy on us!"

you, not a Jew but a Samaritan, are the only one who gives thanks to God. Go on your way. Your faith had made you well."

We had not gone far when a young man came running up to us. "I am a messenger from Bethany," he panted. "I am sent by the sisters Mary and Martha. Their brother, Lazarus, is sick and dying. They wish you to come.

Now we knew that Jesus loved the sisters and their brother. We expected him to be alarmed at hearing that Lazarus was dying, but he calmly said, "This sickness will not end in death, but for the glory of God." And he told the messenger, "I will come when I can."

We then went into the nearest village. "Lord," I said, "do you not care that your friend Lazarus is dying?"

He did not answer. We disciples wondered what

Lazarus was sick.

had come over Jesus. We tarried in that village for two days. On the third day Jesus said we would go to Bethany. "Our friend Lazarus has fallen asleep," he said. "Now I will go waken him."

The journey to Bethany took two days. Before we entered the city, Martha met us on the road, weeping bitterly. "Lord," she said, "if you had been here, my brother would not have died!"

Jesus said, "Your brother will rise to life."

"I know that he will, on the last day," she said.

"I am the resurrection and the life," Jesus said. "Whoever believes in me will live, even though he dies. And whoever lives and believes in me will never die. Do you believe this, Martha?"

"Yes," she said. "I do believe that you are the Messiah!"

Many people were at Martha's house to comfort her and Mary. Some were from Jerusalem, which

"I am the resurrection and the life!"

was less than two miles from Bethany. When Jesus saw Mary and all her friends lost in grief, he was so filled with compassion that he wept. "See how much he loved his friend Lazarus!" someone said.

Then Jesus said to Mary, "Show me your brother's tomb." We went outside the city to a small hill. In the side of the hill was a large stone that covered a hole.

"Take the stone away!" Jesus said.

"But, Lord!" said Martha, horrified. "He has been dead for four days. The smell will be terrible!"

"Did I not tell you that you would see God's glory if you believe?" asked Jesus. Then he said to some men standing near, "Take the stone away." They obeyed silently.

No one spoke. No one even moved. What was Jesus going to do? A look of horror and fear was on everyone's face. The stone was moved. A black pit

"Take the stone away!"

gaped in the hillside. My temples throbbed. Jesus raised his hand. My heart jumped. "Lazarus, come forth!" Jesus said, in a voice that seemed to shake the earth.

Everyone gasped. From out of that dark hole, that tomb, came a man wrapped in the cloths of the dead!

"Praise the name of the Lord!" came the shouts. "The Son of God has come!" News of this spread quickly to Jerusalem.

"Lazarus, come forth!"

They plotted a way to kill Jesus.

11

THE LEADERS' PLOT

We did not know it then, but we learned later that some of the Jews from Jerusalem who had been at Lazarus's tomb went to the priests in Jerusalem and told them what Jesus had done. This made the priests more determined than ever to kill Jesus. They met in a secret council. "If we let this man go on performing miracles like this, all Rome will hear of it," they said. "The Romans will come and take over our beloved temples and destroy our very

religion. We will lose all our power over the people."
And they began plotting a way to kill Jesus.

Somehow Jesus knew of this. He seemed to
know a lot of things before they happened. Many
times he could tell what a person was thinking. Now
we did not go among the Jews, but stayed more and
more in the wilderness. Soon we went north to a
town called Ephraim, where we stayed for a couple
of days before starting for Jerusalem.

On our way we passed through the city of
Jericho. There a man met us in the street. He wore
an expensive robe and gold rings on his fingers. He
recognized Jesus. "Good teacher," he said, "what
must I do to inherit eternal life?"

"Why do you call me good?" Jesus asked. "There
is only one who is good—your Father in heaven.
But if you wish to have eternal life, you must obey

"What must I do to inherit eternal life?"

the commandments. Do not murder, steal, lie, cheat, or commit adultery. Honor your parents and love your neighbors as yourself."

"I have done these things all my life," said the man.

Jesus looked at him with love. "You lack one thing," he said. "Go sell all that you own, give the money to the poor, and then come and follow me."

The man's face fell. He turned and walked away with his head down. Jesus looked after him sadly. Then he said to us, "How hard it will be for the rich to enter heaven! I tell you, it is easier for a camel to pass through the eye of a needle than for a rich man to enter the kingdom of God. Such a man loves his riches more than God."

As we went on, Jesus told again of his coming death. "We are going to Jerusalem," he said. "There

He turned and walked away.

everything written by the prophets about the Son of Man will come true. The chief priests will condemn him to death. He will be tortured and mocked and spit on. They will whip him and kill him. But on the third day he will rise."

We did not understand why Jesus said this, or why it should have to happen as he said, but as we went, a sense of doom seemed to cover us. It hung on us heavily.

A crowd had gathered around us in the street. More and more people joined us. Suddenly Jesus stopped and looked up into a fig tree. A man was sitting in the branches. "Zacchaeus, come down," Jesus said. "I am going to your house today."

The man scrambled down and pushed his way through the crowd. His face was eager, like a child's. But many in the crowd began to scorn him

"Zacchaeus, come down!"

and Jesus. "This man is a tax collector and a cheat," they cried. "How is it that you go to his home and treat him as a friend?"

Jesus shook his head. "I have not come to call the saved, but the lost," he said. "People who are well don't need a doctor, only those who are sick."

Now Zacchaeus, who was very small, led Jesus and us to his house. There he waited on us, bustling about busily. He was awed and overjoyed in the presence of Jesus. "Lord," he said, "I will give half my possessions to the poor." Tears came to his eyes. "And if I have cheated anyone, I will restore his property four times over."

Jesus smiled at him. "Today salvation has come to this house," he said, "to you and all your family."

The days of the Passover celebration were again drawing near, so we set out for Jerusalem. Six days

Zacchaeus repented.

before the Passover, we came to Bethany, where we stayed the night with Lazarus and his sisters.

The next day we started again for Jerusalem. We came to a small village called Bethphage. Before we entered, Jesus sent two of us ahead into the village. "As soon as you enter the village, you will find a donkey tied up," he said. "Untie it and bring it to me. If anyone asks you what you are doing, say, 'The master has sent for this.'"

These two did as Jesus said. Soon they returned with the donkey. Their faces showed awe. "Master!" they said, "it was just as you said it would be!"

Jesus rode this donkey into Jerusalem. Many people were in the city for the Passover. As Jesus entered, crowds flocked to us. "Blessed is the King who comes in the name of the Lord!" they shouted. "Hosanna to the Son of David! Hosanna to the

Jesus rode into Jerusalem.

King of Israel!" And the people cut branches from palm trees and spread these and their cloaks on the ground before Jesus.

We came like this to the temple, and the crowds followed, singing and shouting. The priests looked furious, but they could say nothing. People poured in from the streets. Jesus healed everyone who came to him. "Praise to David's Son! Praise to God!" And the priests gathered in the shadows of the temple and whispered together.

The next morning when we entered the temple, only a few people were there. Now the chief priests came up to Jesus. "Who gave you the right to do these things?" they asked.

"If you can answer one question, I will tell you," Jesus said. "Where did John the Baptist's authority come from, God or man?"

The priests gathered in the shadows.

The priests looked at one another in surprise. Now they began arguing. One said, "If we answer, 'From God,' he will say, 'Why did you not listen to him?' But if we say, 'From man,' there might be rioting in the temple, because the people here all believe John was from God." So they answered, "We do not know."

Jesus said, "Neither will I tell you, then, where my authority comes from."

Now Jesus asked the priests another question. "Tell me," he said, "what do you think? A man had two sons. To one he said, 'Go and work in the vineyard today.' The son said, 'I will not,' but later repented and went. To the other son the man said, 'You too go work in the vineyard.' This son said, 'Yes, sir,' but did not go. Now, which of these sons did the will of his father?"

The priests questioned Jesus.

"The first," said the priests.

"So I tell you," said Jesus, "that tax collectors and harlots are going into the kingdom of God ahead of you. For John the Baptist came to you, showing you the path to take, and you would not believe him. But the tax collectors and harlots did. Even when you saw this, you did not change your minds and believe him.

"Listen to another parable," Jesus continued. "Once a landowner planted a vineyard, which he rented to tenants before he left on a trip. When harvest time came, he sent his slaves to the tenants for his share of the harvest, but the tenants beat the slaves, killing one, and sent the rest back empty-handed. The owner sent more slaves, who were treated the same way. Finally he sent his only son. *Surely they must respect my son*, he thought. But the

The tenants killed the landowner's son.

tenants grabbed the son, beat him, and killed him. Now, when the owner of this vineyard comes, what will he do to those people?"

"He will surely kill those evil men and rent the vineyards to others," said the priests.

Jesus said, "Haven't you read this scripture: 'The stone that the builders rejected as worthless turned out to be the most important one of all'? And so I tell you that the kingdom of God will be taken away from you and given to a people who will produce the proper fruit."

The priests would have arrested Jesus right then, but they were afraid of the people gathering in the temple.

Later, as Jesus was teaching the crowds in the temple, a Pharisee came alone to him. He did not seem to be trying to trap Jesus by questions. Rather,

"Which commandment is the greatest one?"

he seemed to be hungering for the truth. "Teacher," he said, "which commandment in the Law is the greatest one?"

Jesus said, "The most important is this. 'Listen, Israel! The Lord our God is the only Lord. Love the Lord your God with all your mind, and with all your strength.' The second most important commandment is this. 'Love your neighbor as you love yourself.' There is no other commandment more important than these two."

The Pharisee said, "Well spoken, teacher! It is true, as you say, that only the Lord is God, and that there is no other God but he. And man must love God and his neighbor, just as you say. It is more important to obey these two commandments than to offer animals and other sacrifices on the altar to God."

"You are not far from the kingdom."

"You have spoken wisely, my friend," said Jesus. "You are not far yourself from the kingdom of God."

Then Jesus said, in a voice that silenced the whole crowd, "Whoever believes in me believes not only in me but also in him who sent me. I have come into the world as light, so that everyone who believes in me shall not remain in darkness. If anyone hears my message and does not obey it, I will not judge him. I came not to judge the world, but to save it. Whoever rejects me has one who will judge him. The words I have spoken will be his judge on the last day."

Jesus' voice silenced the crowd.

The Passover meal

12

BETRAYAL AND AGONY

It was the Feast of the Unleavened Bread, when the Passover meal was to be prepared. Jesus told us how we were to find a room where we would eat the Passover meal, and it was just as he said. We prepared the lamb, the unleavened bread, and the herbs and spices. When all was ready, Jesus and the rest of the disciples came. We were in a small upper-story room in the heart of Jerusalem.

"I have yearned to eat this meal with you before I must suffer," Jesus said. "I will not eat it again until it is fulfilled in the kingdom of God."

While we were eating, Jesus took off his robe and poured a large bowl of water. Then he got down on his knees and went around the table to each of us. And the Lord, the Son of God, washed our feet and dried them with a towel. "What I am doing you do not understand," he said, "but you will understand later."

When he had finished, he put on his robe and sat with us again. "You call me Lord," he said, "and in this you speak the truth, for that is what I am. Yet I, the Lord, have washed your feet. The Son of Man did not come as 'lord' to be served, as your earthly kings are, but he came to serve. This is how you, too, must serve one another.

"I say this not to all of you, though," Jesus continued. "One of you will betray me!"

"One of you will betray me."

We were startled. "Lord, who is he?" we asked.

"It is one of you twelve, who now eats with me, whom I gave this bread to," he said. He broke a piece of bread and handed it to Judas Iscariot. "Do quickly what you are about to do," he said to Judas. And Judas hurried out of the room. We did not understand this. We thought Jesus had sent Judas on some errand. Only after Jesus' death did we learn that Judas had secretly gone to the chief priest at the temple and offered to betray Jesus. The priests had agreed to pay Judas for his treachery.

After Judas left, Jesus took his wine cup, filled it, and broke a chunk of bread. He handed the bread to each of us. "Take this," he said. "Eat. This is my body, which is broken for you. Do this in memory of me." Then he passed the wine to each of us. "Drink this," he said. "This is my blood, which is poured

Judas hurried from the room.

out for you. This is the blood of a new covenant I am making with you. With my blood I am washing your sins clean.

"And I give you a new command," he said. "You must love one another, just as I have loved you. All the world will know my disciples by their love toward one another. I am going away soon. I am returning to the Father, from whom I came. But I will send the Spirit to you when I am gone. He will come so you will not be alone. And my peace I leave you. You will be filled with my peace."

"Lord," I said, "I am ready to follow you now."

"Peter, I tell you the truth," Jesus said. "Before the rooster crows, you will deny me three times."

"Never, Lord!" I said. There was sorrow and love in my Lord's eyes. "I will never deny you!" I said. "Not even if I have to die with you!" And the other

"Never, Lord!"

disciples swore the same thing.

"My Father's house has many rooms," Jesus said. "I am going to prepare a place for each of you. And you will know where I am going, and you will know the way."

Thomas said, "Lord, we do not know where you are going or the way."

Jesus said, "I am the way, the truth, and the life. No one comes to the Father but through me. If you had known me, you would have known my Father also. And from now on you do know him and have seen him."

Philip said, "Show us the Father! That is all we need."

"For a long time I have been with you," Jesus said. "And yet you still do not know me, Philip? Whoever has seen me has seen the Father. Do you not know,

"I am the way, the truth, and the life."

Philip, that I am in the Father and the Father is in me? This is the truth. The Father and I are one. And whoever believes in me will do what I do—even greater things than I have done. If you remain in me, and my word remains in you, then you may ask me for anything you wish, and you shall have it."

Later that night, after we had sung hymns to God, we went with Jesus out of the city, across the Kidron Valley to a garden called Gethsemane.

Jesus' face was full of something like agony. "Stay here," he said. "I am going to pray." He went off a little way by himself.

The night was very dark and still. The stars shimmered in a clear sky. A fresh, earthy smell filled the garden. It should have been a place of beauty, but that night, to me, the stars glittered like the blades of deadly knives. The earthy

He went off a short distance by himself.

smell of the garden was as suffocating as a grave, and the very darkness of the night hid terrors, crouching, waiting. Something was wrong in the universe. Deathly wrong.

Jesus' voice came to us. There was an agony in it I had never heard from him, or from any man. "Father," he said, "if it is possible, let me not drink of this cup!" Then he came back to us. And his face! What pain I saw there! Sweat poured from him like blood.

"The sorrow in my heart is so great it crushes me," he said. "Stay here and keep watch with me while I pray." He went off again. Listening to his voice, I fell asleep.

"Could you not even stay awake with me for one hour?" The voice woke me. Jesus stood in front of us. The other disciples had also fallen asleep and were

Jesus stood in front of us as we slept.

now waking. A pale light shone in the east.

"But now, look," Jesus said. In the growing light of morning, we saw a large group of men coming toward us. "The hour has come!"

"The hour has come!"

Peter struck with his sword!

13

THE BEGINNING

Now we could see the priests of the temple with many soldiers, led by Judas Iscariot, who came up to Jesus and kissed him. "Hail, Master," Judas said.

"So, Judas," said Jesus, "you betray the Son of Man with a kiss."

The soldiers grabbed Jesus. We later learned that Judas had said, "The one I greet is the one you want."

Now fury rose up in me. I drew my sword and struck at the nearest man, the bondservant of the high priest. My blow cut off his right ear.

"Stop!" said Jesus. "Do you not know, Peter, that if I wished, I could call an army of angels here now, and they would come? This is only happening as it must happen. I am permitting all this." He touched the man's bleeding face and healed him.

Now panic overcame us disciples. We fled, not knowing where to run, or why. But I soon stopped running. Where were they taking my Lord? What would happen to him? I followed the group from a distance.

Jesus was led to an inner courtyard of the temple. There the priests hurled accusations at him. I stopped in an outer courtyard. The morning was cold, and the soldiers had lit a fire. I stood there among the people, warming my hands.

Suddenly someone said, "You are one of his disciples!"

"You are one of his disciples!"

I was terrified. I stammered, "No, I am not."

Soon another man looked at me and said, "You are one of them." Again I denied it. Once more someone saw me and said, "You were with the man, were you not?" And for the third time, I denied it.

Just then I heard the rooster crow. And then I remembered: *Before the rooster crows, you will deny me three times.*

Like a walking dead man, I turned and went out of the temple. As I walked, I began to weep, and my anguish poured from me like blood from my heart. I had denied my Lord, my Savior, my beloved friend! I do not know how long I walked. My heart was cold, my world destroyed. What happened next was a nightmare.

It was the next day. Jesus was in the palace of the governor, Pontius Pilate. Jesus was dressed in a purple robe. A crown of thorns was embedded in

Peter denied the Lord.

his head. Blood seeped from his back through his robe. Soldiers surrounded him. They spit on him and punched him. They cawed and jeered. "Hail to the king of the Jews!" they mocked. He staggered under their blows and winced as they spit in his face. Yet his arms hung at his sides, and his shoulders were stooped.

Jesus stood near Pilate, who was seated on a platform facing a vast crowd of people, most of them Jews. Some in the crowd were weeping, but many more were shouting in fury, "Crucify him! Crucify him!"

The governor stood up. He seemed troubled. "He has done nothing to deserve death!" he said.

The crowd screamed all the louder. "Crucify him!"

"Shall I crucify your king?" cried Pilate.

"We have no king but Caesar!" they shouted.

Jesus stood by Pilate.

"But what crime has he committed?"

"Crucify him! Crucify him!"

Pilate slumped to his chair. He said in a weak voice, "I am innocent of this man's blood."

"His blood will be on our heads, and on our children's heads!" screamed the Jews among the crowd. And the cry of "Crucify him!" grew in pitch and became a chant. Jesus was led away.

He was whipped again with leather lashes in which were tied sharp pieces of bone. The bone pieces ripped out chinks of flesh from his back, chest, and shoulders. Those flogging him seemed possessed. They lashed at Jesus in uncontrollable fury.

When he came out of the city, he was slick with his own blood. It covered him from head to foot. The memory of his words, "My blood is shed for you," cut through me like a sword.

They scouraged Jesus!

Across Jesus' shoulders, tied to his outspread arms, lay a heavy wooden beam, the transept of a cross. He staggered under its weight. Many times he fell. Without his arms to catch himself, he fell on his face, which soon was battered to a pulp. He left a blood-spattered trail behind him as he labored on. The crowd hooted and jeered. No one helped him up when he fell. Sometimes it seemed like hours before he could get to his feet again.

He came like this to a hill called Golgotha, The Place of the Skull. Here he fell and could not rise. Now the soldiers threw him onto the upright of the cross. They drove long spikes through his wrists and ankles into the hard wood. Then they lifted the cross and dropped it into place.

Over Jesus' head was an inscription that Pilate had ordered carved: THIS IS JESUS OF NAZARETH, KING OF THE JEWS.

The walk with the cross

And on that day—on that hill—evil was a living, crawling thing. It writhed through the crowd like a snake. People screamed insults at the bloody figure on the cross. "Save yourself! Come down from the cross!" The soldiers cast lots on the ground, gambling for Jesus' robe, which lay on the ground.

At midday, suddenly the sky became dark as night. The looks of wild hatred froze on the faces of those nearest the cross. No one moved. No one spoke. I heard only my heart beating.

The darkness hung over the whole land for three hours. Then Jesus cried out in a blood-choked voice, "My God, my God, why have you abandoned me?" His breath came in shallow, ragged grasps. He was drowning in blood from his battered chest. I could hear him talking faintly, "Father, forgive them, for they do not know what they are doing." Then his head slumped forward. He was dead.

"My God, my God, why have you abandoned me?"

Then the earth came alive. The ground shuddered under our feet. The shudder became a rumble, and the rumble became a roar. All the earth shook as if in fury. Great boulders on the hillsides cracked and split apart and tumbled downhill.

The crowd scattered in every direction. Doughty soldiers wailed like babies in terror. People beat their breasts and pulled their hair as they reeled over the trembling ground.

And from within the heart of the temple came a shrieking, rending sound. The massive curtain leading to the Holy of Holies was ripped like paper from top to bottom. The two ragged pieces hung like corpses.

Three days later, the eleven of us found one another and met in the room where we had eaten the Passover meal with our Lord. We nursed our grief

The earth shook.

together late into the evening.

We had come to believe in him as the Messiah, the Promised One. And then he was murdered on a cross!

Our door was locked that night. We had reason to hide. The priests hated us as his disciples. We talked about what to do, where to go now.

Suddenly a figure entered the room, right through the door! We gasped.

"Peace to you," said a familiar voice. Jesus!

"A ghost!" we screamed.

The figure walked up to us. "Does a ghost have flesh and bone?" he said. "Touch me. Do you not remember that I told you I would rise on the third day?"

In awe, we each touched his hands, his face. There were jagged scars on his wrists. He was the same, yet different. He was stronger, brighter, as if

"Peace to you!"

death had tempered him like steel in fire.

We were overcome by joy! We knelt and worshipped him. "My Lord and my God!" we cried.

He stayed with us many hours that night, and he came to us several times after that. On the day he left us, he reminded us that he would return in the Spirit. "Go now into all the world and make everyone my disciple," he said. "And I will be with you always, until the end of all things."

It was not the end, but only the beginning.

"I will be with you always!"

CHRONICLES OF FAITH
BIBLE DICTIONARY

Abraham   The ancestor of the Israelite people. God promised him that his descendants would be God's people forever.

apostle   This means "to send forth." Jesus sent his disciples "into all the world" to preach the news about him.

baptize   The beginning, or birth, of a new life and the death of an old life. John baptized people in the water to show a washing of their sins. Jesus said we must be "born of the spirit" to enter heaven. This means we must receive a new life from God, who is spirit.

church   The body of Jesus Christ on earth. His believers all over the world are his body.

covenant   A sworn agreement between two people, or a promise made by God to man. God made a covenant with Abraham when he promised that Abraham's descendants would always be his people. Jesus Christ made a new covenant with all mankind when he gave his life as a sacrifice for our sins.

demon   A spirit and follower of Satan. Demons, like Satan, were once angels. When Satan rebelled against God, God banished Satan from heaven. A third of the angels—now called demons—are said to have followed Satan.

disciple A devoted follower. In Jesus' day, the Jewish teachers of the Law had disciples to whom they taught all the details of the Law. Jesus called twelve men to be his disciples. They were to leave everything behind and follow Jesus wherever he went. A disciple now means anyone who accepts Jesus Christ as Lord and Savior and follows him throughout life.

Herod Roman king of Judea when Jesus was born. He was not popular with his subjects

because he was not a Jew himself and was faithful to Rome,
the Jews' conquering nation. He
sought to kill Jesus when Jesus
was an infant. Herod had heard
of Jesus' birth and how Jesus
was called the "King of the
Jews," which was Herod's title.
Herod died about two
years after Jesus was born.

**Holy of
Holies**

The innermost shrine of
a Jewish temple. The most
significant of these was the one
in the temple of Jerusalem, the
capital of Judea. This shrine was

considered sacred. No one but the high priest could enter here, and he only once a year. It was believed that here the high priest had access to God himself. At Jesus' death, God tore the curtain that covered the entrance of the Holy of Holies to show that Jesus is now the only access to God the Father.

hosanna   A shout of praise to God. It means, "Save, we ask."

Messiah   In Hebrew this meant

"anointed." In Greek, the language used most widely in Jesus' day, it was "Christos," or "Christ." To the Jews it meant the anointed king of Israel. The Jews expected a king who was chosen by God, who would rule not only Judea, but all of Israel. Jesus is that king. As the angel Gabriel said to Mary (see chapter 2), "There will be no end to his kingdom."

parable   A story used to explain a truth or principle. Jesus spoke in parables so that his message would be received by those whose hearts were ready to receive it. God's truth cannot be received in our understanding, but only in our hearts. Jesus said his words are spirit and life. The life his words bring to us must begin, or be born, in our hearts. This is what Jesus meant when he said, "You must be born of the Spirit."

Passover A yearly ritual celebrated by the Jews in memory of their escape from slavery in Egypt under Moses' leadership.

Pharisee   In Jesus' day, Pharisees were
Jews who had made a compli-
cated system of laws based on
God's Ten Commandments.
The Pharisees believed a person
could become holy only by
strict obedience to their laws.

Pilate,   Roman governor of Judea from
Pontius   A.D. 26 to A.D. 36. He was
not king but presided over
matters of Roman law. The
Jewish leaders failed to con-
vince him that Jesus had
committed any crime under
Roman law. (Rome did not

recognize Jewish law.) Then the leaders claimed Caesar, ruler of all Rome, as their only king. They said this to imply that Pilate would make himself an enemy of Caesar's if he freed someone (Jesus) who also claimed to be king. Finally the Jewish leaders stirred up the crowd to such a frenzy that Pilate yielded Jesus to them out of fear of a riot.

Samaritan   A person who lived in the region of Samaria, just north of Judea. The Jews hated the

Samaritans because the
Samaritans, originally from one
of the twelve tribes of Israel,
had intermarried with
foreigners and practiced other
religions.

scourge   To punish by whipping.
Sometimes this was done to the
death. The cat-o'-nine-tails,
used to beat Jesus, was a whip
of nine leather cords, each tied
into a knot. The wounds left
by this whip looked like the
clawings of a cat. Sometimes,
out of particular cruelty, sharp

pieces of bone were tied into these knots, making the cuts much deeper and more painful. Jesus was whipped with these bone pieces.

synagogue A place for Jewish worship and religious study. Here the Jewish leaders taught from the scriptures.

Tabernacles, Feast of the In Hebrew, tabernacle meant "dwelling." This was a sacred tent, which God instructed the Israelites to make during their trek through the desert after escaping from Egypt. The origin of the feast is not clear, but may have been a symbolic renewal of God's covenant with Israel.

THE CHRONICLES OF FAITH SERIES

Exciting stories and action-packed illustrations
for 8- to 12-year-old readers. . .
only $4.97 each!

ELIJAH
ISBN 978-1-59789-923-9

The life of the powerful,
miracle-working prophet.

JOSEPH
ISBN 978-1-59789-926-0

The story of a slave boy
turned ruler of Egypt.

ESTHER
ISBN 978-1-59789-924-6

A powerful story of
courageous leadership.

PAUL
ISBN 978-1-59789-927-7

The life of the great missionary,
Bible writer, and miracle worker.

JESUS
ISBN 978-1-59789-925-3

The story of the Son of God
in His life and ministry on earth.

RUTH
ISBN 978-1-59789-928-4

A story of great faithfulness in
the midst of hardship.

Available wherever Christian books are sold.